Why you cannot impeach Donald Trump.

The source of the strength for Donald Trump

Chapter 1: Introduction

I am a medical doctor born in Burundi, my beloved and great nation located in Africa specifically in East Africa.

After my birth at hospital, my dearest father was asked what name he wanted me to be called. He said:"Nizigiyimana" meaning" In God we trust ".

In other words, I was cast on God the creator of Heaven and the earth since my birthday. Hope you understand why I love the great people of America because of their "In God we trust" slogan.

Burundi has an ethnical issue - like hatred between my beloved

The source of the strength for Donald Trump

great people Hutu and my beloved great people Tutsi- that had been pulling down the country for many years instead of going forward.

I thank God I have been protected from being under influence of stereotypes against my different ethnical people.

The great Burundi has three (3) different types of people called:" Hutu, Tutsi and Twa." They are all great. I love my father and mother because they never talked to me about Hutu people as my enemies. His friends are Hutu and Tutsi. I grew up in that atmosphere of loving all people including the great people who used to be neglected in Burundi, my beloved and great people of Twa. Whether minority or majority we are all

The source of the strength for Donald Trump

one people that must live together as one great nation one Burundi.

At university there were two (2) blocks of Hutu and Tutsi. Tutsi students would find themselves almost alone without Hutu and so Hutu students would find themselves almost alone without Tutsi among them.

You know what? I would go among the Hutu students and make them my friend and they were always asking me:" Who are you? I am a child of God. Maybe when they looked at me they could see me looking like Tutsi but they were confused because I was always with them some time and some time with Tutsi students. I am proud of that behavior.

A human being is a human being! I have to love everybody! Why hating a human being like you? Why not desiring to see other people doing well like you? When you practice love you are promoting yourself!

I used to say to myself I am Hutu, I am Tutsi, I am TWA. All of them are my beloved people and I am proud of that. I stayed in a house with Hutu people my people. One of them I used to call her as my "mother." That great woman of God but late now used to take care of me like her beloved son. She was a woman who loved to help people. Her husband -who used to beat her because she was not giving birth to male children- before he passed away, used to call her "UNHCR United Nations High Commissioner for Refugees." because she was helping everyone. And the more

The source of the strength for Donald Trump

she helps other people the more God continued to make her richer. I thank God for having given her later a son, who came as a "savior" to her against the unfounded hate of her husband.

One day that mother wanted to pay for me the school fees at a private university but I did not get a place and continued at the public University called "the University of Burundi." She was ready for anything that can make me happy. Her children are like my sisters and my brother. You see how blessed I was? God can use a very person for your goodness that is why it is not good to despise other people. You do not know who has been ordained to take you to your destination. That is a secret of God unless it is revealed unto you. There is a reason why you

The source of the strength for Donald Trump

are with someone together for the first time or many times, be grateful for that and talk to each other nicely.

Therefore, stop limiting yourself and lock up to yourself in your small tribe, race, nation... Start seeing yourself as a world citizen. No matter how rich your nation maybe it is not a reason to cut relationship with so called poor nations as long as they are human beings like you. They have hands you may need ; therefore look how you can help them to get developed like you because you will find that you are making yourself more developed and more richer.

Today in Zambia the people that are strengthening me or blessing me are not Burundians or members

The source of the strength for Donald Trump

of my family but they are people of this wonderful nation of Zambia. Be thankful to God for who you are and be grateful to God also for your brothers and sisters who are black or white because God created people with different skin colors for your own good and happiness. Love everyone!

My prayer is to see *One Rwanda one People"* and one *Burundi one Nation* like what my beloved and great people of Zambia a great nation with more than 73 tribes did as *"One Zambia one Nation. "*

Imagine if we form one nation great nation where all nations from all over the world are found themselves and use English as an official language just to unite all the

The source of the strength for Donald Trump

nations under one King and always before the news we hear "One world one nation" like in my great beloved people of Zambia. Imagine if we are united as one powerful nation through ties of love to each other and make great our great world nation! Only in this way we are going to overcome poverty and wars between nations because there will be no more of "this is my territory, this is our water". There will be no need of nuclear weapon that my beloved and great people of Iran and North Korea are trying by all means to possess like other powerful nations.

My beloved and great people of China, Russia and United States of America will be working together as one people with the entire whole world developing

The source of the strength for Donald Trump

all together including my beloved and great people of Africa. Those trillions of US dollars we are spending in military will be spent against poverty. There will be no space war at all because the space belongs to all of us. Why fight for the things we did not create?

Zambia is not ashamed in their tribes. It is an easy thing to ask a tribe of a Zambian which is not easy in Burundi or Rwanda. When I see people who resemble Tutsi or Hutu in Burundi or Rwanda in Zambian people and they do not hate each other because their noise like in Burundi or Rwanda.

If in Zambia they cannot hate and kill each other because of their noise why not stop that

The source of the strength for Donald Trump

stupidity of killing each other for generations in Burundi and Rwanda forever and build a strong nation without any hatred based on the appearance of somebody's noise. Enough is enough!

Forget the killing in the past and come together and form one strong new Burundi one people and one strong new Rwanda, one people. *Choose forgiveness and love one another.*

I do not like to be in one box. Every human being is my friend my brother, my sister. Black, White, Chinese, people Asiatic… as long as they are human beings I love them and they are my people. They can feel hungry like me, they can be happy like me therefore we as human beings

The source of the strength for Donald Trump

are one and must live together as one and help each other as one world great nation without borders. A world without egoism. A world that shares technology easily with other nations because we are all human beings condemned to better our lives with dignity.

At university, one of my friends was a Hutu and very intelligent, Hutu people have been into power for many years in Burundi.

If you want to overcome some of stereotypes you have accepted effortlessly because of what you heard against other people from your different leaders or ancestors, it is easy and you will always find that what you were told is a fake information and that there is no reason of hating each other.

The source of the strength for Donald Trump

13 I remember when I took oath as a medical doctor in Burundi, I held the Burundian flag by faith as a "world flag". All nations are my people. I am a medical doctor for all nations and I am proud of that.

I like to watch news not of the local news but also international news. Why? I want to know what is happening around the globe. I am concerned of what happening around the globe and think what can be done as solution to different issues. Today God has made our world too small to live without knowing what happening around the globe almost instantly. We are in the right time of gathering all nations of our beautiful world into one great nation.

The source of the strength for Donald Trump

14 → A friend of mine asked me one day why I like to watch those international news through these great main media like CNN, FOX news, France 24; Aljazeera... where they show almost only the bad news. "I want to know what is happening around the world with my people from all over the world so that I can pray for them." I replied to her. I believe prayer is powerful because God does perform miracles through prayers!

"Why have you come to work at our clinic? Is it not to wait for the patients who are coming with their health issues and give a solution for them to come out of their bad conditions?" I asked her again. She kept quiet like someone convinced.

15 →

People should not fear to watch news nationally and internationally for them to be a solution to the different people of our beloved and great world. You can pray for any problem that is emerging in any part of the world and bring a change. And the Father in heaven who sees in secret will reward you! The time will never allow you to be isolationist! What is hitting in South Arabia is also hitting the global economy. As the whole world, we form one body, it Hurricane is hitting America it is also hitting the whole body: The whole world!

When I was first called David?

When I was 11 years old, I was given a new name in my local Pentecostal church in an area called Kibenga right in the

The source of the strength for Donald Trump

Capital city of Bujumbura. What's that?"David" was the new name given to me. Jesus says "I tell you the truth, whatever you forbid on earth will be forbidden in heaven, and whatever you permit on earth will be permitted in heaven." Matthew 18:18, <u>New Living Translation</u>.

So that name given in my great church was also permitted in heaven.

A certain Sunday that I will never forget I asked one of the leaders to give a time to testify how I got born again. As small as I was, the pulpit was taller than me then they had to put me on the drum for me to be able to speak facing the audience holding the microphone in my hands. At the end of my testimony, a man of God who was leading said:" You are David".

The church started calling me "David". In other words, the man of God said you are like David the one who fought against Goliath in the name of the Lord Yahweh and won using a stone and a slinger without a sword in his hands.

David cut off his head and later on became a king after the heart of God over the Israel who was the people of God in all the Earth before Jesus died for all nations for all generations. Hope you understand why I love the people of Israel as my own people and Arabs people because they share one ancestor "Abraham".

These great people they are brothers. They must love each

The source of the strength for Donald Trump

other between themselves and between them and all Christians because all the people became children of Abraham through our dearest Jesus the MESSIAH! Whether you believe it or not you cannot change it. A car is a car whether you believe it or not!

While at University in the medical faculty, I put on that name of "DAVID" cheerfully and wholeheartedly. I received the spirit of David I said to my God who is the Father of the Whole World:'' *Heavenly Father may you use me seven times the same way you used King David in his time in the name of Jesus Christ but protect me from the weakness of King David and those of King Solomon. I want to make a difference! Both King David and King Solomon did something that*

The source of the strength for Donald Trump

19

gave occasion to the enemies of the LORD to blaspheme. I even told the Lord to make me wiser and wealthier than king Solomon and keep me from doing wrong against his laws. I want to shame the devil. In short, I want to please my Lord Jesus Christ by making a difference. I want to be a rich king through holy ways and still love God and His people as a husband of one wife. I want badly to change what King Solomon did. I do not know why but that it is a burden in me!

I give myself to you Lord Jesus to rule like your king David over all nations because you died for all nations without exception of any nation around the globe in your name of Jesus Christ!"

20

I started reading the bible to know who David whose name means "beloved" was.

As, I was reading the bible I found out that the same way I was cast to the Lord and pushed to trust in God through my surname from my mother's breast, King David also was pushed to trust in the Lord since his mother's breast: *"Yet you brought me out of the womb; you made me trust in you, even at my mother's breast. From birth I was cast on you; from my mother's womb you have been my God."*Psalm22:10, New International Version (NIV).

Why this resemblance? I always ask myself. Simple coincidence? I know that nothing happen by accident.

21 Another resemblance with King David: When my mother was still alive, she is the one who used to share the word of God at home. She would organize how to pray. She was committed in serving the Lord. She used to sing in a choir and she liked that so much. I used to escort her when she was going to visit different people at their place and share the Word of God with them. She was my really my friend and I loved her a lot.

The way I was too closed to my mother was the same connection that King David had with his mother. How I know that?

That is very simple question because King David said:*"Truly I am your servant, LORD; I serve you just as my mother did; you have freed me from my chains.*" Psalm 116Psalm116:16, New International Version.

That means that King David was most connected to his mother than to his father. The bible does not tell us about the mother of David. Why David was the person behind the sheep of his father? Why the father forgot about him when the prophet of the Yahweh came to anoint one of his sons to become king of Israel to unseat King Saul?

I used to wonder why until I read the following article about the mother of King David by this great woman Chana Weisber

The source of the strength for Donald Trump

Nitzevet, Mother of David

The bold voice of silence

Save me, O God, for the waters threaten to engulf me. . .

I am wearied by my calling out, and my throat is dry. I've lost hope in waiting. . .

More numerous than the hairs on my head are those who hate me without reason. . .

Must I then repay what I have not stolen?

Mighty are those who would cut me down, who are my enemies without cause. . .

O God, You know my folly, and my unintended wrongs are not hidden from you. . .

The source of the strength for Donald Trump

24 →

It is for your sake that I have borne disgrace, that humiliation covers my face.

I have become a stranger to my brothers, an alien to my mother's sons.

Out of envy for Your House, they ravaged me; the disgraces of those who revile you have fallen upon me. . .

Those who sit by the gate talk about me. I am the taunt of drunkards. . .

Disgrace breaks my heart, and I am left deathly sick.

I hope for solace, but there is none; and for someone to comfort me, but I find no one.

They put gall into my meal, and give me vinegar to quench my thirst. . . (Psalm 69)[1]

The source of the strength for Donald Trump

This psalm describes the life of a poor, despised and lowly individual, who lacks even a single friend to comfort him. It is the voice of a tormented soul who has experienced untold humiliation and disgrace. Through no apparent cause of his own, he is surrounded by enemies who wish to cut him down; even his own brothers are strangers to him, ravaging and reviling him.

Amazingly, this is the voice of the mighty King David, righteous and beloved servant of God, feared and awed by all.

King David had many challenges throughout his life. But at what point did this great individual feel so alone, so disgraced, and so undeserving of love and friendship?

The source of the strength for Donald Trump

26 What caused King David to face such an intense ignominy, to be shunned by his own brothers in his home ("I have become a stranger to my brothers"), by the Torah sages who sat in judgment at the gates ("those who sit by the gate talk about me") and by the drunkards on the street corners ("I am the taunt of drunkards")? What had King David done to arouse such ire and contempt? And was there no one, at this time in his life, which would provide him with love, comfort and friendship?

This psalm, in which King David passionately gives voice to the heaviest burdens of his soul, refers to a period of twenty-eight years, from his earliest childhood until he was coroneted as king of the people
of Israel by the prophet Samuel.

The source of the strength for Donald Trump

27

David was born into the illustrious family of Yishai (Jesse), who served as the head of the *Sanhedrin* (supreme court of Torah law), and was one of the most distinguished leaders of his generation. Yishai was a man of such greatness that the Talmud (Shabbat 55b) observes that "Yishai was one of only four righteous individuals who died solely due to the instigation of the serpent"— i.e., only because death was decreed upon the human race when Adam and Eve ate from the Tree of Knowledge at the serpent's instigation, not due to any sin or flaw of his own. David was the youngest in his family, which included seven other illustrious and charismatic brothers.

The source of the strength for Donald Trump

28 ➤ Yet, when David was born, this prominent family greeted his birth with utter derision and contempt. As David describes quite literally in the psalm, "I was a stranger to my brothers, a foreigner to my mother's sons. . . they put gall in my meal, and gave me vinegar to quench my thirst."

David was not permitted to eat with the rest of his family, but was assigned to a separate table in the corner. He was given the task of shepherd because "they hoped that a wild beast would come and kill him while he was performing his duties,"[2] and for this reason was sent to pasture in dangerous areas full of lions and bears.[3]

Only one individual throughout David's youth was pained by his

The source of the strength for Donald Trump

unjustified plight, and felt a deep and unconditional bond of love for the child whom she alone knew was undoubtedly pure.

This was King David's mother, Nitzevet bat Adael, who felt the intensity of her youngest child's pain and rejection as her own.

Torn and anguished by David's unwarranted degradation, yet powerless to stop it, Nitzevet stood by the sidelines, in solidarity with him, shunned herself, as she too cried rivers of tears, awaiting the time when justice would be served. It would take twenty-eight long years of assault and rejection, suffering and degradation until that justice would finally begin to materialize.

David's Birth

The source of the strength for Donald Trump

Why was the young David so reviled by his brothers and people?

To understand the hatred directed toward David, we need to investigate the inner workings behind the events, the secret episodes that aren't recorded in the prophetic books but are alluded to in Midrashim.[4]

David's father, Yishai, was the grandson of Boaz and Ruth. After several years of marriage to his wife, Nitzevet, and after having raised several virtuous children, Yishai began to entertain personal doubts about his ancestry. True, he was the leading Torah authority of his day, but his grandmother Ruth was a convert from the nation of Moab, as related in the book of Ruth.

The source of the strength for Donald Trump

During Ruth's lifetime, many individuals were doubtful about the legitimacy of her marriage to Boaz. The Torah specifically forbids an Israelite to marry a Moabite convert, since this is the nation that cruelly refused the Jewish people passage through their land, or food and drink to purchase, when they wandered in the desert after being freed from Egypt.

Boaz and the sages understood this law—as per the classic interpretation transmitted in the "Oral Torah"—as forbidding intermarriage with converted *male* Moabites (who were the ones responsible for the cruel conduct), while exempting female Moabite converts. With his marriage to Ruth, Boaz hoped to clarify and

The source of the strength for Donald Trump

publicize this Torah law, which was still unknown to the masses.

Boaz died the night after his marriage with Ruth. Ruth had conceived and subsequently gave birth to their son Oved, the father of Yishai. Some rabble-rousers at the time claimed that Boaz's death verified that his marriage to Ruth the Moabite had indeed been forbidden.

Time would prove differently. Once Oved (so called because he was a true *oved*, servant of God), and later Yishai and his offspring, were born, their righteous conduct and prestigious positions proved the legitimacy of their ancestry. It was impossible that men of such caliber could have descended from a forbidden union.

The source of the strength for Donald Trump

However, later in his life, doubt gripped at Yishai's heart, gnawing away at the very foundation of his existence. Being the sincere individual that he was, his integrity compelled him to action.

If Yishai's status was questionable, he was not permitted to remain married to his wife, a veritable Israelite. Disregarding the personal sacrifice, Yishai decided the only solution would be to separate from her, no longer engaging in marital relations. Yishai's children were aware of this separation.

After a number of years had passed, Yishai longed for a child whose ancestry would be unquestionable. His plan was to

The source of the strength for Donald Trump

34 ➤ engage in relations with his Canaanite maidservant.

He said to her: "I will be freeing you conditionally. If my status as a Jew is legitimate, then you are freed as a proper Jewish convert to marry me. If, however, my status is blemished and I have the legal status of a Moabite convert forbidden to marry an Israelite, I am not giving you your freedom; but as a *shifchah k'naanit*, a Canaanite maidservant, you may marry a Moabite convert."

The maidservant was aware of the anguish of her mistress, Nitzevet. She understood her pain in being separated from her husband for so many years. She knew, as well, of Nitzevet's longing for more children.

The source of the strength for Donald Trump

35 → The empathetic maidservant secretly approached Nitzevet and informed her of Yishai's plan, suggesting a bold counter plan.

"Let us learn from your ancestress and replicate their actions. Switch places with me tonight, just as Leah did with Rachel," she advised.

With a prayer on her lips that her plan succeeds, Nitzevet took the place of her maidservant. That night, Nitzevet conceived. Yishai remained unaware of the switch.

After three months, Nitzevet's pregnancy became obvious. Incensed, her sons wished to kill their apparently adulterous mother and the "illegitimate" fetus that she carried. Nitzevet, for her part, would not embarrass her husband by

The source of the strength for Donald Trump

revealing the truth of what had occurred. Like her ancestress Tamar, who was prepared to be burned alive rather than embarrass Judah, [5] Nitzevet chose a vow of silence. And like Tamar, Nitzevet would be rewarded for her silence with a child of greatness who would be the forebear of <u>Moshiach</u>.

Unaware of the truth behind his wife's pregnancy, but having compassion on her, Yishai ordered his sons not to touch her. "Do not kill her! Instead, let the child that will be born be treated as a lowly and despised servant. In this way everyone will realize that his status is questionable and, as an illegitimate child, he will not marry an Israelite."

The source of the strength for Donald Trump

37 ➤ From the time of his birth onwards, then, Nitzevet's son was treated by his brothers as an abominable outcast.[6] Noting the conduct of his brothers, the rest of the community assumed that this youth was a treacherous sinner full of unspeakable guilt.

On the infrequent occasions that Nitzevet's son would return from the pastures to his home in Beit Lechem (Bethlehem), he was shunned by the townspeople. If something was lost or stolen, he was accused as the natural culprit, and ordered, in the words of the psalm, to "repay what I have not stolen."

Eventually, the entire lineage of Yishai was questioned, as well as the basis of the original law of the Moabite

The source of the strength for Donald Trump

convert. People claimed that all the positive qualities of Boaz became manifest in Yishai and his illustrious seven sons, while all the negative character traits from Ruth the Moabite clung to this despicable youngest son.

Anointing King David

We are first introduced to David when the prophet Samuel is commanded to go to Beit Lechem to anoint a new king, to replace the rejected King Saul.

Samuel arrives in Beit Lechem, and the elders of the city come out to greet him, nervous at this unusual and unexpected visit, since the elderly prophet had stopped circulating throughout the land. The elders feared that Samuel had heard about a grievous sin that was taking place in their city.[7] Perhaps he had come to rebuke them over the behavior of Yishai's despised shepherd boy, living in their midst.

Samuel declared, however, that he had come in peace, and asked the elders, and Yishai and his sons, to join him for a sacrificial feast. As an elder, it was natural for Yishai to be invited; but when his sons were inexplicably also invited, they worried that perhaps the prophet had come to publicly reveal the embarrassing and illegitimate origins of their brother. Unbeknownst to them, Samuel would anoint the new king of Israel at this feast. All that had been revealed to the prophet at this point was that the new king would be a son of Yishai.

The source of the strength for Donald Trump

40 → *When they came, Samuel saw Eliav (Yishai's oldest son), and he thought, "Surely God's anointed stands before Him!"*

But God said to Samuel, "Don't look at his appearance or his great height, for I have rejected him. God does not see with mere eyes, like a man does. God sees the heart!"

Then Yishai called Avinadav (his second son), and made him pass before Samuel. He said: "God did not choose this one either."

Yishai made Shammah pass, and Samuel said, "God has not chosen this one either."

Yishai had his seven sons pass before Samuel. Samuel said to Yishai, "God has not chosen any of them."

The source of the strength for Donald Trump

At last Samuel said to Yishai, "Are there no lads remaining?"

He answered, "A small one is left; he is taking care of the sheep."

So Samuel said to him, "Send for him and have him brought; we will not stir until he comes here."

So he sent for him and had him brought. He was of ruddy complexion with red hair, beautiful eyes, and handsome to look at.

God said: "Rise up, anoint him, for this is the one!" (I Samuel 16:6-12)

The Small One, Left Behind

As Samuel laid his eyes on Yishai's eldest son, he was certain that this was the future

The source of the strength for Donald Trump

king of Israel. Tall, handsome and distinguished, Eliav was the one whom Samuel was ready to anoint, until God reprimanded Samuel to look not at the outside but at the inside.[8]

No longer did Samuel make any assumptions of his own, but he waited to be told who was to become the next king. All the seven sons of Yishai had passed before Samuel, and none of them had been chosen.

"Are these all the lads?" Samuel asked. Samuel prophetically chose his words carefully. Had he asked if these were all Yishai's *sons*, Yishai would have answered affirmatively, that there were no more of *his sons*, since David was not given the status of a son?

The source of the strength for Donald Trump

43 ➤ Instead, Yishai answered, "A small one is left; he is taking care of the sheep." David's status was small in Yishai's eyes. He was hoping that Samuel would allow David to remain where he was, out of trouble, tending to the sheep in the faraway pastures.

But Samuel ordered that David immediately be summoned to the feast. A messenger was dispatched to David who, out of respect for the prophet, first went home to wash himself and change his clothes. Unaccustomed to seeing David home at such a time, Nitzevet inquired, "Why did you come home in the middle of the day?"

David explained the reason, and Nitzevet answered, "If so, I too am accompanying you."

The source of the strength for Donald Trump

As David arrived, Samuel saw a man "of ruddy complexion, with red hair, beautiful eyes, and handsome to look at." David's physical appearance alludes to the differing aspects of his personality. His ruddiness suggests a warlike nature, while his eyes and general appearance indicate kindness and gentility.[9]

At first Samuel doubted whether David could be the one worthy of the kingship, a forerunner of the dynasty that would lead the Jewish people to the end of time. He thought to himself, "This one will shed blood as did the red-headed Esau."[10]

God saw, however, that David's greatness was that he would direct his aggressiveness toward positive aims. God commanded Samuel, "My anointed one is

The source of the strength for Donald Trump

standing before you, and you remain seated? Arise and anoint David without delay! For he is the one I have chosen!"[11]

As Samuel held the horn of oil, it bubbled, as if it could not wait to drop onto David's forehead. When Samuel anointed him, the oil hardened and glistened like pearls and precious stones, and the horn remained full.

As Samuel anointed David, the sound of weeping could be heard from outside the great hall. It was the voice of Nitzevet, David's lone supporter and solitary source of comfort.

Her twenty-eight long years of silence in the face of humiliation were finally coming to a close. At last, all would see that the lineage of her youngest son was pure, undefiled by any blemish. Finally, the anguish and humiliation that she and her son had borne would come to an end.

Facing her other sons, Nitzevet exclaimed, "The stone that was reviled by the builders[12] has now become the cornerstone!" (Psalms118:22)

Humbled, they responded, "This has come from God; it was hidden from our eyes" (ibid. verse 23).

Those in the hall cried out in unison, "Long live the king! Long live the king!" Within moments, the once-reviled shepherd boy became the anointed future king of Israel.

Nitzevet's Legacy

King David would have many more trials to face until he was

The source of the strength for Donald Trump

acknowledged by the entire nation as the new monarch to replace King Saul. During his kingship, and throughout his life, up until his old age, King David faced many ordeals.

King David possessed many great talents and qualities which would assist him in attaining the tremendous achievements of his lifetime. Many of these positive qualities were inherited from his illustrious father, Yishai, after whom he is fondly and respectfully called *ben Yishai,* the son of Yishai.

But it was undoubtedly from his mother that the young David absorbed the fortitude and courage to face his adversaries. From the moment he was born, and during his most tender years, it

The source of the strength for Donald Trump

was Nitzevet who, by example, taught him the essential lesson of valuing every individual's dignity and refraining from embarrassing another, regardless of the personal consequences. It was she who displayed a silent but stoic bravery and dignity in the face of the gravest hardship.

It is from Nitzevet that King David absorbed the strength, born from an inner confidence, to disregard the callous treatment of the world and find solace in the comfort of one's Maker. It was this strength that would fortify King David to defeat his staunchest antagonists and his most treacherous enemies, as he valiantly fought against the mightiest warriors on behalf of his people.

The source of the strength for Donald Trump

49

Nitzevet taught her young child to find strength in following the path of one's inner convictions, irrespective of the cruelty that might be hurled at him. Her display of patient confidence in the Creator that justice would be served gave David the inner peace and solace that he would need, over and over again, in confronting the formidable challenges in his life. Rather than succumb to his afflictions, rather than become the individual who was shunned by his tormentors, David learned from his mother to stand proud and dignified, feeling consolation in communicating with his Maker in the open pastures.

She demonstrated to him, as well, the necessity of boldness while pursuing the right path.

The source of the strength for Donald Trump

When the situation would call for it, personal risks must be taken. Without her bold action in taking the place of her maidservant that fateful night, the great soul of her youngest child, David, the forebear of Moshiach, would never have descended to this world.

The soul-stirring psalms composed by King David in his greatest hours of need eloquently describe his suffering and heartache, as well as his faith and conviction. The book of Psalms gives a voice to each of us, and has become the balm to soothe all of our wounds, as we too encounter the many personal and communal hardships of life in *galut* (exile).

The source of the strength for Donald Trump

As we say these verses, our voices mesh with Nitzevet's, with King David's, and with all the voices of those past and present who have experienced unjustified pain, in beseeching our Maker for that time when the "son (descendant) of David" will usher in the era of redemption, and true justice will suffuse creation.

FOOTNOTES

1.

Translation taken from *The Living Nach*, published by Moznaim.

2.

Siftei Kohen, Vayeishev.

3.

See I Samuel17:34-36

The source of the strength for Donald Trump

52 →

<u>4.</u> The story and concepts in this chapter are based on *Yalkut HaMachiri*, as well as *Sefer HaTodaah* (section on Sivan and Shavuot). See also an interesting English rendition in the book *Don't Give Up*, pp. 187ff.

<u>5.</u>

See Genesis ch. 38, and Midrashim and commentaries on that chapter.

<u>6.</u>

In the verse in the psalm where David says he was a "stranger" to his brothers, the Hebrew word for stranger, *muzar*, is from the same root as *mamzer*—bastard, illegitimate offspring.

<u>7.</u>

The source of the strength for Donald Trump

> **53** Commentaries of Radak and Abarbanel to 1 Samuel16:3.

<u>8.</u>

A short while after this coronation feast, David was instructed by his father to visit Eliav at the battlefield. A war with the Philistines was imminent, and Eliav lashed out in anger at David. This tendency to anger disqualified Eliav now from the throne. (This event occurred after David was anointed as king. However, according to the commentaries, it is possible that they didn't understand the implications of the anointing, assuming that Samuel had designated David as a new student in his school of prophecy. Though this was an honor, and an act that would validate David's lineage, only

The source of the strength for Donald Trump

once David actually became king over the entire nation did his brothers realize his true greatness.)

9.

Malbim.

10.

Bereishit Rabbah 63:8.

11.

Midrash Tanchuma, Va'eira 6.

12.

The Hebrew word in this verse for "builders," *bonim*, is the same root as the word for "sons.

The key of David in my hands

In the book of Isaia55:3- 5 we read:"

Give ear and come to me;
    listen, that you may live.
I will make an everlasting
covenant with you,
    my faithful love promised to
David.
See, I have made him a
witness to the peoples,
    a ruler and commander of the
peoples.
 Surely you will summon
nations you know not,
    and nations you do not know
will come running to you,
because of the Lord your God,
    the Holy One of Israel,
    for he has endowed you with
splendor." New International
Version.

The source of the strength for Donald Trump

56 I was then stirred up by the Holy Spirit to receive those promises from God. Jesus said that when we ask we have to believe we have received.

Another word says that the descendants of David will lead like God , like angel of God.

On that day the LORD will shield those who live in Jerusalem, so that the feeblest among them will be like David, and the house of David will be like God, like the angel of the LORD going before them. Zechariah 12:8, New International Version.

Through Christ I am a descendant of David. Therefore this promise is mine. I will rule like God, like Jesus and like an angel of God.

The source of the strength for Donald Trump

57 The bible says also that Jesus has he keys of David.

But What is the key of David and what does it symbolize?

Well. The key of David appears only twice in the Bible. The first time it appears is in Revelation where it states, "To the angel of the church in Philadelphia write . . . who holds the KEY OF DAVID" (Revelation 3:7). The speaker is the resurrected Jesus, whom John sees in a vision, and the message is to the church at Philadelphia. The possession of this key by Christ is used as proof that the being addressing the church is God, "the Holy One, the One Who is true."

The second occurrence of the key of David is in the book of Isaiah the prophet where it

The source of the strength for Donald Trump

states, "And the key of the house of David will I lay upon his shoulder (Eliakim as an allusion or type of Christ); so he shall open, and none shall shut; and he shall shut, and none shall open" (Isaiah 22:22, KJV).

In short the key of David in the hands of Jesus means Power and authority, the ability to unlock or lock something.
  Since the descendants of David will rule like God and we know that Jesus is God. Therefore I will rule holding the keys of David as well.

You can ask before I continue :" Is Jesus really God?". The answer is yes like what I said in the book:" One world , one nation under one God, Jesus Christ."

Jesus is God of gods and Lord of lords.

One day I was discussing with a friend of mine who was a member of Jehovah witness. He was telling me that Jesus is not God the creator. He used some scriptures and I demonstrated that Jesus is the only true God the creator of the universe as described in the holy bible. When I showed him another scripture that proved him wrong, he said:" I am going to rethink about that."The devil knows that once we acknowledge Jesus as God and not as a mere prophet like Moses and Elijah, then we have won over him.

The source of the strength for Donald Trump

60 *Jesus is the Jehovah but who came in the world with a human body in the name of Jesus. In the plan of God was to reveal himself to His created and teach them how to worship the true God, their maker. Before Jesus came, God used Moses, prophets as the mediator between a man and God. They were human beings and therefore they were imperfect vessels of God. There was a need of a perfect one who is God himself. And that was His majesty Jesus Christ the living True God.*

Water that is pure and passes through an impure pipe becomes contaminated with some impurity. The water is no longer pure and it is not good for health.

Our heavenly father used to send human beings to teach his law

The source of the strength for Donald Trump

like Moses and other prophet like the Prophet Elijah but they were like imperfect pipe, imperfect vessels. God had to come down himself in the name of Jesus Christ to teach us how to love him and worship in the proper manner.

Jesus was without sin because He is God. He was not from Adam. Jesus asked Pharisees:" Can any of you prove me guilty of sin? If I am telling the truth, why don't you believe me? John 8:46, New International Version.

You cannot remove a sin while yourself you have sins. So Jesus because He was God therefore He was the right one to come in the world and take away the sin of the world caused by the rebellion of Adam.

The source of the strength for Donald Trump

He is from heaven, from God himself. In the book of Luke 1:35 . We read:"The angel answered and said to her (Mary the mother of Jesus), "The Holy Spirit will come upon you and the power of the Most High will overshadow you; and for that reason the holy Child shall be called the Son of God.

It appears at John 1:29, where John the Baptist sees Jesus and exclaims, "Behold the Lamb of God who takes away the sin of the world."

Jesus knew and defended that He was God. Jesus, in response to the Pharisees' question "Who do you think you are?" said, "'your father Abraham rejoiced at the thought of seeing my day; he saw it and was glad.' 'You are not yet fifty years old,' the Jews

The source of the strength for Donald Trump

said to him, 'and you have seen Abraham!' 'I tell you the truth,' Jesus answered, 'before Abraham was born, I am!' At this, they picked up stones to stone him, but Jesus hid himself, slipping away from the temple grounds" (John 8:56–59). The violent response of the Jews to Jesus' "I AM" statement indicates they clearly understood what He was declaring—that He was the eternal God incarnate. Jesus was equating Himself with the "I AM" title God gave Himself in Exodus 3:14.

If Jesus had merely wanted to say He existed before Abraham's time, He would have said, "Before Abraham, I was." The Greek words translated "was," in the case of Abraham, and "am,"

64

in the case of Jesus, are quite different. The words chosen by the Spirit make it clear that Abraham was "brought into being," but Jesus existed eternally (see John 1:1).

There is no doubt that the Jews understood what He was saying because they took up stones to kill Him for making Himself equal with God (John 5:18). Such a statement, if not true, was blasphemy and the punishment prescribed by the Mosaic Law was death (Leviticus 24:11-14). But Jesus committed no blasphemy; He was and is God, the second Person of the Godhead, equal to the Father in every way.

To the all my beloved and great people who are in Judaism and Islam, I would like to show again that the God of Jacob, the

The source of the strength for Donald Trump

God of Abraham has been revealed to the World in the name of Jesus Christ.

In the book of _Revelation 22:13_ Jesus said to Apostle John:"I am the Alpha and the Omega, the first and the last, the beginning and the end."; we read also in _Revelation 1:8_:"I am the Alpha and the Omega," says the Lord God, "who is and who was and who is to come, the Almighty."; _Revelation 21:6_ :"Then He said to me, "It is done I am the Alpha and the Omega, the beginning and the end I will give to the one who thirsts from the spring of the water of life without cost."

Let me also add the verses respectively _Revelation 1:17_ and _Revelation 2:8_ :"When I saw Him, I fell at His feet like

The source of the strength for Donald Trump

66

a dead man And He placed His right hand on me, saying, "Do not be afraid; I am the first and the last, "And to the angel of the church in Smyrna write: The first and the last, who was dead, and has come to life, says this:"

In the old testament we find that Jesus is the same in old testament and the new testament when we read in the book of Isaiah where the God of Jacob called himself like the First and the Last:"

Isaiah 44:6"Thus says the LORD, the King of Israel and his Redeemer, the LORD of hosts: 'I am the first and I am the last, and there is no God besides Me.

Isaiah 48:12"Listen to Me, O Jacob, even Israel whom I

The source of the strength for Donald Trump

called; I am He, I am the first, I am also the last.

Isaiah 41:4"Who has performed and accomplished it, Calling forth the generations from the beginning? 'I, the LORD, am the first, and with the last I am He.'""

These verses demonstrate that Jesus is the Same God in the Old Testament and in the New Testament.

Jesus is given the name of Lord of lords in the New Testament which is also found in the Old Testament meaning that Jesus Christ is the same God in the Old Testament and in the New Testament:

Proof in the New Testament

In Revelation 19:16 we read:"On his robe and on his thigh he has

The source of the strength for Donald Trump

68 ➤ *a name written, King of kings and Lord of lords." And we read also in Revelation 17:14 They will make war on the Lamb, and the Lamb will conquer them, for he is Lord of lords and King of kings, and those with him are called and chosen and faithful."*

Proof of the calling of God the Lord of lords from the Old Testament.

Deuteronomy 10:17:" For the Lord your God is God of gods and Lord of lords, the great, the mighty, and the awesome God, who is not partial and takes no bribe.";

Psalm 136:2-3: "Give thanks to the God of gods. His love endures forever.

The source of the strength for Donald Trump

69 ➤ *Give thanks to the Lord of lords,*

For his steadfast love endures forever;"

This is the proof that our beloved Lord and Savior Jesus Christ is the same God in the Old Testament and the New Testament. He is the God of gods; the God of Abraham, Isaac and Jacob who created us and who deserves and he only worship forever and ever. There is no power, no king, and no lord who can oppose Him and win! Hallelujah! Halleluiah!

Shame the devil by your worship while kneeling down

Satan always look the best that God always look for because he

The source of the strength for Donald Trump

70

knows what that is the best God desires a lot that moves His heart.

When Satan was tempting he told Jesus:" If you bow down and worship me, I will give all the kingdoms of the earth!" But our always overcomer, our good friend Jesus Christ rebuked Satan and said:" It is written you shall worship God and serve Him only!"

This kind of worship is the best that the devil was looking from His Creator Jesus Christ for Satan to grant to Jesus the kingdoms of the world.

asking for Jesus to

I like to worship my Lord Jesus Christ and spend some times before the Lord kneeling down as a sacrifice of thanksgiving for

The source of the strength for Donald Trump

71

having died for me and the whole world just to shame the devil.

One day I ask a certain pastor:" Here in Zambia you like to kneel down to show a respect to someone who deserve honor but how many times do you kneel down when you are praying God?"

It is no easy to kneel down; it is painful. Then I understood why to kneel down in worship to God is the best because it is a sacrifice in its own.

One night I was praying and took more than one hour praying kneeling down to shame the devil and I heard a voice saying like:" If you worship me and bow down before me, I will make everything bow down to you!" In order words God will make turn a "none" into a "yes". He will

The source of the strength for Donald Trump

make disobedient people obedient by His power.

He will make what is impossible possible. He will make all rulers of the earth obey and serve me! God instructed princes through the prophet of God Ezechiel to bow down in worship while in temple! If you do not have your legs, you can still worship God in your heart because the true worshipper God is looking for is a person who worships God in true and in Spirit and that means worship out of your heart.

God is interested by a true worship from your heart expressed physically knelling down or lifting up your hands as a sign of surrender the own Moses used to overcome the enemy while Joshua was on the ground

The source of the strength for Donald Trump

fighting against the enemy. Any revelation that worked in the past was also revealed to us in our time. But the Holy Spirit is the one who can lead you what kind of weapon you need to use in prayer for a particular situation.

My beloved people from all the world let's spend some times kneeling down in worship before the King of kings our Lord, and God Jesus Christ and give this kind of worship to Jesus for the glory of our heavenly Father and bring shame to the devil.

The source of the strength for Donald Trump

Key of David used for the victory of Donald Trump in 2016

I am used using the keys of David to resolve some issues against the will of God. Before I speak about my beloved and great man Donald Trump, a man who likes to keep his words. I

The source of the strength for Donald Trump

used the power behind the keys of David for Ben LADEN BEFORE Donald Trump.

Do you want to know how?

The end of Osama Ben Laden

How did I use the key of David I understood that when God has given you something it is already there that is why He said believe that you have already received whatever you ask for. That means in Heaven they know they have already a King over all the Earth who comes in the name of Jesus. When I gave myself to our beloved Heavenly Father in the name of Jesus Christ, I said:" Lord here I am, send me Lord I am ready to rule the whole world like your David king in my time"

76 ➤ After that The Holy Spirit led to a verse I had not yet known before written in Zechariah14.9: "The Lord will be king over the whole earth. On that day there will be one Lord, and his name the only name." New International Version. When I saw this prophecy I realized I am under a divine mission to fulfill this prophecy.

In the time Of David the throne of David was also a throne of God; His kingdom was The Lord's. That is why God said I watch over your kingdom why? Because it was His. So the success of the David in what right in the eyes of God was God's therefore it was impossible to fail for David. The Lord made sure he succeeded where he went and became more powerful than his enemies.

The source of the strength for Donald Trump

77

We are in the right time for the Lord to be king over all the earth through me. There is television; the time has come for the ruling of his king David in his name.

Another vow I did to the Lord Jesus Christ is to remove all idols once a King. After that vow, the Holy Spirit led me to a prophecy written in Zechariah 13Zechariah13.2: "On that day, I will banish the names of the idols from the land, and they will be remembered no more," declares
the Lord Almighty. "I will remove both the prophets and the spirit of impurity from the land. New International Version. I understood that all those vows are inspired by the Holy Spirit to do his will on the Earth.

The source of the strength for Donald Trump

78 I understood I am sent by heaven to establish His kingdom on Earth and to do his will on earth as it is in heaven. In heaven there is only one God, no other idols. If God is for me who can be against me? It is a divine agenda. God always stir up a man to fulfill divine purpose. We are in the time of God and He will make sure He succeeds because no man can obstruct his purpose.

Let me tell you another strange thing happened in Burundi:

A powerful man of God the late Dr Myles Munroe came in Burundi before in his last days of life. He was preaching in the Church called Living Church of Jesus Christ". Suddenly, I heard a voice in me:" This man is going to die". I said maybe it

The source of the strength for Donald Trump

is just a voice! After Burundi he went in Kenya, and I was told that in Kenya he said: "My mission here on earth is over. I am empty I am ready to go back home. After those words his private jet crashed." He died with his wife. Then I remembered the voice. I couldn't believe he really died. I remembered that what I said if David a prophet that meant God will use also as his prophet.

What Dr Myles Munroe used to preach was to teach people to establish the Kingdom of God on Earth. Why God is he foretelling me his death? Maybe because what he was preaching to people it was a burning dream to apply what he was teaching all over the world.

The source of the strength for Donald Trump

Was Dr Myles Munroe my forerunner or was he like John to Jesus?

His key verse was contained in The prayer of our Lord and God Jesus to his disciples, when you pray say:" Our heavenly Father, Hallowed be your name, may your kingdom come! May your will be done on the earth as it is in heaven!

What is the name that Jesus was talking about that must be honored on the earth? Of course the name of Jesus Christ. What? Yeah, when Jesus was praying: he said: Father, I protected those you gave me in your name you gave me. The name of Jesus! Jesus and the Father they are one.

When Apostle Paul was still called Saul persecuting the

The source of the strength for Donald Trump

81 →

followers of Jesus , He caught him by force and Saul asked? Who are you Lord? He answered: "I am Jesus you are persecuting. Meaning Jesus is ruling like a lion but not like a lamb. A lion is in charge of the jungle. It is not a democracy it is a kingdom!

In psalm 2:8-9 Jesus asked David his king: *"If you ask, I will give you nations, everyone will be yours. You will rule them with great power, you will scatter your enemies like broken pieces of pottery.''*

I remember one day I said my dear Lord Jesus Christ, I believe in every word you have written or say. That is why I said that I have asked nations and they are mine they are my people and I started loving and

The source of the strength for Donald Trump

82 →

praying for all nations as my beloved people.

I started stared following what is happening around our dear globe. I intercede for the world as my own people as one people. When others are busy praying for their own nation, my concern is the whole world including. The world is now like a small village.

In 2001, right on our Television, what was happening was horrible: The 9/11, the "black" day to USA. The great nation in the world full of intelligent people, full of nuclear weapons and all kind of arms was beat and hit by mere human beings. My beloved American people were injured of a group of people. The bible says "*If the LORD does not build*

The source of the strength for Donald Trump

the house; it is useless for the builders to work on it. If the LORD does not protect a city, it is useless for the guard to stay alert." Psalm 127:1 (GW)

It was not an attack only to USA but to the Whole world.

In 2011, I was in my praying room right in Bujumbura, and the Spirit took over me and I said with all my heart: Lord, remember that anyhow America is a nation according the forefathers of USA used Bible for the constitution. Most of missionaries are from USA all over the world like those I worked with in the Burundi at a hospital of kibuye where I operated as a replacer of a medical whom doctor American in the Pediatric service.   I was very happy to work with them.

The source of the strength for Donald Trump

84 Those guys were good and hardworking. They helped a lot the people of that region Of Burundi in the province of Gitega.

I remember Dr John a tall man, who was operating as ophthalmologist. One day Dr John asked me:"

Where did you get English from? Have you ever travelled? I negatively replied him.

In Burundi we speak French but these days we also speak English because Burundi is also in East Africa community. But I wanted to know English because it is like English is known almost all over the world. So English help to connect with people from all over the world. When I am speaking English I want to speak like American maybe that is why

The source of the strength for Donald Trump

some American friends tell me I speak well English.

So attack America meant to attack me it is like to attack Israel as well. I love America and I love Israel too.

So, in my room I said Lord, if you gave me the key of David: what I open no one can shut what I shut no one can open. This a prayer that I used to confess even when I am with others, and one of my friend told me : It is not what you are asking that everybody can ask there is something what God has put on your heart that will be your own burden but not for everybody. I remember what the Savior of the Whole World said: "You cannot receive this saying unless, to whom it is given. " Matthew 19Matthew19.11.

The source of the strength for Donald Trump

Then I prayed America is like to attack Christianity, those who attacked America came in the name of a religion; and then I said: Lord Jesus let Ben Laden be captured by America. If America it is Christ who wins, but if not then Islam would think they won. I SHOUTED: "IN THE NAME OF Jesus Christ I arrest Ben Laden!"

Some days I heard that Ben Laden was died. What happened It was only God who used those intelligent soldiers.

Obama was pushed by a hand behind the scene .The Hand of God. There were not sure of victory, Obama was advised by his men not to go for the mission because it was really risky.

The source of the strength for Donald Trump

I advice all my beloved human beings liked me who are in Islam to love Christ Jesus like their God and Savior. Only him He is worthy of worship all over the World!

Trump VICTORY

During 2016 US elections this great woman Hillary Clinton had a bigger support than Trump. Hillary was supported by Obama. Hillary had a lot of Money in her campaign more than Trump. Hillary had the main media behind her while Trump was not. He chose to use Facebook and Tweeter.

I like Obama but I hated what He did in supporting homosexuality instead of helping our beloved people under the bad spirit of homosexuality to get rid of it so that instead of adopting children because they were created to have children of their own through heterosexuality. Homosexuality is a sickness and the world must fix it. When you support a sin you became weak. Hillary was not saying against homosexuality meaning she was going to continue what Obama was doing.

Obama is married to his lovely wife Michelle Obama why not help others who are in the wrong way to become normal like him? I read on internet that if you support homosexuality vote Hillary but if not vote Trump.

I said: "Lord Trump must win in the name of Jesus Christ. If you made the first born of all rulers oh Lord, then I allow Trump to win. I started following polls. When I was

The source of the strength for Donald Trump

89

praying Trump would go up in the polls but when not praying Hillary, that courageous lady would lead the polls.

That remembered what happened with Moses whenever he would raise his hands in prayer Israel would win but when not the enemy would lead the battle. Moses was on the mountain praying while Joshua was the commander on the ground but all eyes were on Moses. Aaron, the brother to Moses realized that, He put Moses on a stone and help Moses to hold his hands up until the total victory.

When I realised how things were going on. I started praying continually until the day before the general elections. Trump won because God was for him. My beloved people in Democrats were

The source of the strength for Donald Trump

surprised of the victory. They think it is the president Putin of my beloved great people of Russia who became wiser than Obama in refusing homosexuality that Obama was supporting that enabled Trump to win.

It is Jesus Christ was against you! Homosexuality is a serious sin that brings a curse to people and defile the earth and whoever is supporting it is an enemy of the people because he is helping them to their auto destruction. You are annihilating their future generation in them. Jesus is the same in the time of Sodom and Gomorrah, today and forever. I love Obama. He is courageous brilliant, intelligent but I did not like the support for protecting a sin instead of fighting to find out a way to

The source of the strength for Donald Trump

91 → help and save our beloved people under the spirit of homosexuality.

But do you know there is a reward to people who follows and fight for the righteousness of God? Jesus Christ the Savior of the Earth said that "happy are those who are pure in the heart for they shall see God" meaning they shall experience the miraculous salvation from God, they shall see his power in their life.

I am a witness for that how righteousness benefit everyone who practices it! Do you want to know about my experience? :

When I reached Zambia, my visa was about to expire, I rushed to the border to renew my visa. The government had already given me a letter that allow me to serve

The source of the strength for Donald Trump

92

my beloved great Zambian people as their medical doctor but an immigration officer wanted me to give them some money. For what? Corruption?

''If you don't have the money then I will put in jail!'' The chief intimidated me. I told him I do not have the money they asking me. They were working for the government of this great man, a man I love who declared October 18th of every year a "national prayer day", the president Edgar c. Lungu which government had accepted to give me a job but these people was acting against the government.

They wanted me to give them $300 and they pushed me to pay them quickly otherwise the following day I would pay $400. You know what? The $300 was the exact

The source of the strength for Donald Trump

money for the license from the healthy profession council of Zambia? A friend of mine heard already promised to pay that money for the license. When they heard there is someone who is ready to pay that money, they told me to call him and bring them the money. I called friend and he said that he was going to come the following day. They told me while we are waiting for your friend we are going to put in a hotel.

But, the chief called and told me:" Here there is no comedy, you pay the money or we put in jail!"

"Sir, I told you I do not have money now but if the Lord God to put me in jail pleases do it! "I replied him fixing my eyes to him without fear.

The source of the strength for Donald Trump

94 →

"I am done", the chief commanded a woman immigration officer who tried to look for a way to save me from the chief but in vain. May God bless and guide in the ways of the righteousness all women from all over the World!

They put me in a police cell with other Zambians who were there some because of a crime they committed and other foreigners who were there because they entered Zambia without passport, without visa.

An immigration officer who took me to the cell told me He is going to put in the cell while they are waiting for the money.

"It is a command from the chief otherwise you do not deserve the cell." The immigration officer explained to me.

The source of the strength for Donald Trump

In the cell everyone liked me and they wondering why they put me there. It was a small room with a lot of people. I felt compassion for those people.

Once in the cell they started getting a lot of food from different people more than what they were getting before me.

"Doctor abwera bwino (meaning This doctor has Come with blessings)!"One of my friends in the cell told his friend using the Zambian local language.

This is the same thing my beloved Aunt and her great husband told me once I was already in Zambia. They told me that I was a source of blessing to them while I was staying with them at their home. I stayed with them for many years up to the day I left Burundi to

The source of the strength for Donald Trump

96 ➤ Zambia. Her husband, a great man that I love prayed for me the night before I left Burundi. That unforgettable night tears came out of my eyes. I was going to miss them!

My dearest own father told me you are "Nizigiyimana" (meaning in God I trust) God will be with you! I am grateful to my dearest wonderful and Almighty heavenly Father for choosing my father as my biological father! He is a man of faith!

What they said what the Lord Jesus promised me:

"All nations shall serve you and they shall be blessed through you!

They will pray for you and bless you.

The source of the strength for Donald Trump

In your time righteousness and prosperity shall abound!"

I give you my righteousness and my justice. Leaders will bring you gifts will bring you precious gifts…"psalm72:1-end

When I was in the cell people told me that pray God that the your friend come quickly otherwise you will go in the court after some 1or 2 months like us and you are not going to win in the court because you are a foreigner.

Thank you for telling me that. I said whether my friend comes or not I will come out here as a free man.

I prayed:" remember my God that I have been praying for Zambia

The source of the strength for Donald Trump

as my own people starting to the president Lungu;

Remember also I did not commit adultery when that man wanted to pay for me an Indian prostitute woman in Zambia because it was a sin to you (although there is a pleasure but it is not a right pleasure. It is something that takes someone to auto destruction.)

Therefore my God do not allow them to put me in court and let me leave this cell as a free man without any my handcuffs on my hands.

Another thing in the in the cell it was hot. I wanted to bath but there was no water. The only water that was there was for the chief within the cell.

The source of the strength for Donald Trump

"Unless water is coming out of the tab inside the cell, all of these people cannot bath." One of my friend Burundian but entered Zambia as a Congolese who was crossing Zambia toward South Africa the land of the late Nelson Mandela, gave me the condition for me to bath. He was there for two months.

I prayed: "Lord, I want to bath, please let the water comes through the tap so that I can bath and change the climate; Remove hotness in the cell all the time I am in the cell!"

In the evening, it rained (it was a rainy season but the day I visited the cell it was not raining for some days. The sun was hitting seriously Lusaka the capital of the great Christian nation of Zambia) and the water

The source of the strength for Donald Trump

100 ➤ came out of the tap. All the prisoners went to bath one by one! I was happy the answer to my prayer that was benefiting other people as well. They were blessed through me God is faithful where you are. His promises are yes and amen through Christ. I love the way our beloved Jesus Christ the God of gods and Lord of lords is faithful. I love righteousness.

Can I tell you that the hotness disappeared from that day up to the day I left the cell on the fifth day? Our God is awesome! The night before the fifth day which was the last day in the cell, I was reading Psalm71 where David was asking God to give a command and save him.

*"Be my rock of refuge,
    to which I can always go;*

The source of the strength for Donald Trump

*give the command to save me,
     for you are my rock and my
fortress." Psalm71:3. New
International Version.*

Then I heard the Holy Spirit telling me:"give a command yourself to come out of the cell!" I ten commanded in the name of Jesus as I was told.

You can't believe that early in the morning of the fifth day of my visitation in that dark "world", I heard people calling me:'' Burundian wake up you are called by an immigration officer!" I was released without going in the court what amazed a policeman who asked me:"How come you are released without going in the court?"; others left the place with handcuffs but me nothing was on my hands I left the cell as a free man back to

The source of the strength for Donald Trump

town with a new visa without paying any money according to my prayer to my beloved God in whom I trust. People in the cell, Zambians were happy I was released. They loved me.

They were truly my friends! I advised them during the last night to behave well honoring God in the society once they are released. Like Joseph in prison I was respected in the cell. In the same night I talked to them that some of them were going to be released miraculously the following day.

The day I was made free there 2 young men who were released miraculously and they praised God and told me:" God is big!", "yes He is". I agreed with them! Maybe I was sent in the cell for them and for the release of all so called foreigners that I found there because none of them remained there! I like to see people are happy; I love the people, the sheep of God! Jesus said to Peter if you love me take care of my sheep!

I praise my heavenly father for have put climate in my hands in the name of Jesus. The key of David was working perfectly: "to open and no one can shut, to shut and no one can open."I praise also my savior and my rock Jesus Christ for remembering my righteousness and saved from the hands of that immigration officer in charge who escorted when I was released. Was he apologizing? I don't know but we separate peacefully and I told him: "Thank you and God bless you!"

The source of the strength for Donald Trump

What is making Trump strong

Amid controversy over a summer phone call between US President Donald Trump and the new leader of Ukraine, House Speaker Nancy Pelosi ordered a formal impeachment inquiry of the US president in September.

"No one is above the law," she said as she announced the House was moving forward with an official impeachment inquiry of Trump.

Pelosi, a Democrat, had earlier resisted calls to begin impeachment proceedings, urging

The source of the strength for Donald Trump

restraint as House committees aggressively investigated Trump, a Republican, through subpoenas of witnesses and documents.

But following allegations that Trump pressured the leader of Ukraine to investigate the family of former Vice President Joe Biden, who is vying for the 2020 Democratic presidential nomination, pressure from inside the Democratic caucus for an impeachment inquiry mounted.

Since then, three House committees have held closed-door hearings, deposing current and formal officials who were close to the dealings at the centre of the inquiry.

The House on Thursday is expected to approve ground rules for moving forward with public hearings.

106 →

Here is what you need to know about the US impeachment:

1. What is impeachment in the US political system?

The founders of the United States included impeachment in the US Constitution as an option for removal of presidents by Congress.

Impeachment, a concept in English common law, was one of the more hotly debated points during the constitutional convention of 1787 in Philadelphia. Delegates agreed that presidents could be removed if found guilty by Congress of "treason, bribery or other high crimes and misdemeanors".

The sole authority under the Constitution to bring articles of impeachment is vested in the

House of Representatives where proceedings can begin in the Judiciary Committee. If the House approves articles of impeachment, or "impeaches" a president, he or she would then be subject to trial in the US Senate.

2. On what grounds can a president be impeached? How does impeachment work?

Under the Constitution, the president, vice president and "all civil officers of the United States" can be removed from office for "treason, bribery, or other high crimes and misdemeanors".

To begin impeachment proceedings, a House member can introduce an impeachment resolution, or the entire House can vote to initiate an

The source of the strength for Donald Trump

investigation into whether there are grounds for impeachment. The House Judiciary Committee or a special committee will then investigate. The panel votes on whether to bring a vote to the full House. Impeachment in the 435-member House must be approved with a simple majority.

If the House votes to impeach, the matter moves to the Senate, where a trial is held. The chief justice of the US Supreme Court presides over the trial.

A two-thirds majority vote is required in the 100-member Senate to convict and remove a president from office.

The Senate is made up of 53 Republicans, 45 Democrats and two independents who caucus with the Democrats. At least 20

109

Republicans would have to vote with all Democrats and the two independents to remove the president.

3. Which presidents have been impeached?

Only two US presidents have ever been successfully impeached and in neither instance was the president removed from office. Andrew Johnson was impeached in 1868 in the tumultuous aftermath of the American Civil War; and Bill Clinton in 1998 for issues including his relationship with White House intern Monica Lewinsky. Both times, the House approved formal charges and impeached the president, only to have the Senate fail to convict and remove him.

The House Judiciary Committee in 1974 voted to recommend

The source of the strength for Donald Trump

110

impeachment accusing another president, Richard Nixon, of planning to obstruct an investigation in the Watergate scandal. Before the full House could vote on impeachment, Nixon became the only US president ever to resign. https://www.aljazeera.com/news/2019/05/impeachment-6-190510153644885.html

The source of the strength for Donald Trump

111

One may ask a question what makes really Trump stronger until now. Nothing happens by change. Things have a way to be done. There are some rules that are universal for everyone.

The source of the strength for Donald Trump

In the book of Isaiah54:14, we read:" In righteousness you will be established…"New International Version (NIV).

That means that when you do what is right before the Lord God our heavenly Father you become strong because God is backing you up. You become powerful because the Almighty God has endorsed you. How? God can back you through prayer like what I am doing for Trump using the key of David in the name of Jesus Christ the redeemer of all nations.

When I see what Donald Trump is doing I do not doubt His success even against impeachment. He is a human being but his strength is that he tries to stand for what God loves. When you stand for Jesus God stands for you.

The source of the strength for Donald Trump

113 That makes your enemies hard to overcome you if they are not hurt.

First all I would start by his desire to see the American people more prosperous in creating more jobs. What you have is what you give. As a father fight for His children that is how Trump is making sure that all Americans are well treated. He is making sure that his people are well fed in bringing more companies home.

When Jesus was on earth, He would feed His people. Therefore when your dream is to create jobs , bringing opportunities to people; it means you are trying to make sure your people are fed by giving what they can give them enough money for them using their hands and skills.

The source of the strength for Donald Trump

114

That mindset makes you stronger because you are fighting for the interest of people as a good father. The love always makes people stronger because God always support caregivers thinking good for His people that Jesus died for.

I was happy also when I read what my beloved and great Donald Trump is doing for Christ.

President Trump is Committed to Protecting Religious Freedom in the United States and Around the World

Quote:

Each of us has the right to follow the dictates of our conscience and the demands of our religious conviction.

The source of the strength for Donald Trump

President Donald J. Trump

ADVANCING RELIGIOUS FREEDOM AROUND THE WORLD: President Donald J. Trump is putting religious freedom on center stage at the United Nations.

President Trump is hosting the Global Call to Protect Religious Freedom event, calling on the international community and business leaders to work to protect religious freedom.

The President is calling on all nations to act to bring an end to religious persecution and stop crimes against people of faith.

The State Department has hosted two Religious Freedom Ministerials, during which more than 100 governments and

The source of the strength for Donald Trump

religious leaders committed to fight religious persecution.

The Administration is spearheading the International Religious Freedom Alliance, an alliance of nations dedicated to confronting religious persecution around the world.

The Administration has taken steps to protect victims of all faiths from religious violence.

The Administration will dedicate an additional $25 million to protect religious freedom and religious sites and relics.

The Department of Justice hosted its Summit on Combating Anti-Semitism in July.

The United States has provided humanitarian aid to help Christians and Yazidis who suffered at the hands of ISIS

The source of the strength for Donald Trump

117

and to help Rohingya Muslim refugees fleeing persecution.

SAFEGUARDING RELIGIOUS FREEDOM AT HOME: President Trump has made it a priority to support every American's fundamental right to religious freedom enshrined in the Bill of Rights.

In 2017, President Trump signed an executive order to advance religious freedom, restoring the ideals that have undergirded our Nation since its founding.

The President took action to ensure Americans and organizations are not forced to violate their religious or moral beliefs by complying with Obamacare's contraceptive mandate.

The Department of Health and Human Services (HHS) established a new Conscience and Religious Freedom division to help direct the agency's efforts to protect religious freedom.

HHS took action to protect the right of healthcare entities to act according to their conscience.

This year, the Administration finalized a rule providing more flexibility for Federal employees whose religious beliefs require them to abstain from work on certain days.

The Administration has unequivocally stood for religious freedom in the courts.

COMBATING A GLOBAL CRISIS: The Trump Administration's efforts to advance religious freedom are vital to combating rising levels of violence around the globe.

119 → Eighty-three percent of the world's population lives in nations where religious freedom is threatened or banned.

The Trump Administration is deeply concerned for the more than 1 million Uighurs interned in Chinese internment camps.

Christians are the most persecuted religious group in the world.

Jews, Christians, Muslims, Buddhists, Hindus, Sikhs, Baha'is, humanists, and non-believers alike—almost every group has been increasingly persecuted over the past decade. "

https://www.whitehouse.gov/briefings-statements/president-trump-committed-protecting-religious-freedom-united-states-around-world/.

The source of the strength for Donald Trump

120

Another thing Trump is doing is to fight for the voiceless people like the unborn people. According to Reuters (Published: 5:48am, 19 Jan, 2019) "US President Donald Trump spoke in a pre-recorded video to thousands of anti-abortion activists in Washington on Friday for the 46th March for Life, vowing to veto any legislation that "weakens the protection of human life". That is a courageous for the voiceless people in the womb of their mothers who are supposed to protect with all their strength before even an outsider intervene like President Trump. That makes Donald Trump stronger.

Remember what Jesus said:"He who has found his life will lose it, and he who has lost his life for

The source of the strength for Donald Trump

My sake will find it." Matthew 10:39, New American Standard Bible.

That means to fight for a life of innocent people like unborn babies, those weak people. God is for them and whenever you fight for them you are fighting for God and Jesus said: "And the King will say, 'I tell you the truth, when you did it to one of the least of these my brothers and sisters, you were doing it to me!' Matthew 25:40, New Living Translation.

When Donald Trump is fighting for those precious sisters and brothers that are still in the womb, it means that he is fighting for the King of life Jesus Christ the creator of the mankind.

The source of the strength for Donald Trump

Jesus told Saul that the people he was persecuting represented Himself. Apostle Paul after being changed from Saul into Paul reported what happened that day with Jesus in Acts 26:14:"We all fell to the ground, and I heard a voice say to me in Aramaic, 'Saul, Saul, why do you persecute Me? It is hard for you to kick against the goads.'"

Trump is fighting against persecution against Christians. He is fighting a divine war. That makes Donald Trump backed by heaven. "If God is for you who can be against us? It is written in Romans 8:31.

Donald Trump is fighting the Lord's battles AND God because of His faithfulness will fight for Him. There is a promise of

The source of the strength for Donald Trump

God in Isaiah41:11-12 for people who is standing for what is right. _"All who rage against you

will surely be ashamed and disgraced;
those who oppose you
will be as nothing and perish.
[12] Though you search for your enemies,
you will not find them.
Those who wage war against you
will be as nothing at all.
[13] For I am the LORD your God
who takes hold of your right hand
and says to you, Do not fear;
I will help you."

That is why I want to tell all my beloved democrat people and all my beloved and great people of America to honor and respect Donald Trump because if God is

The source of the strength for Donald Trump

with him you will never win. Remember when America was fighting against ISIS, our beloved and great people were happy because they saw themselves backed by America, a nation that God made powerful for a reason.

But when Donald Trump removed the brave US American soldiers from Syria because he wanted to keep his promise at all cost of removing, our beloved Kurds people found themselves helpless. They were powerful when America was there. Imagine how powerful you are when God is with you.

If he was trying to investigate what caused the Ukrainian prosecutor to be removed from his position because he was fighting corruption, I think it

The source of the strength for Donald Trump

is a wise thing because he is trying to stand for justice. I think we should support that. If there is nothing against my beloved and great man Joe Biden then it is okay and that will make him stronger. I think we should cerebrate what Trump is doing. Otherwise it is like you are protecting our beloved man Joe Biden from a particular crime.

Stand with Donald Trump while He is looking for a way to make America and keep America great.

I would like to end this small book by telling you the vision I had when I was praying in my room concerning the new world order as a holy world holy nation for Christ where New York is like the new Jerusalem as capital city of the new world

The source of the strength for Donald Trump

order under one God Jesus Christ.

God bless America and all the nations including Kurds our beloved people that must preserved as a part of our body.

May Peace, prosperity, righteousness and justice of our Lord God in the name of Jesus be the portion for the entire world. I love you and I pray for you!

The source of the strength for Donald Trump